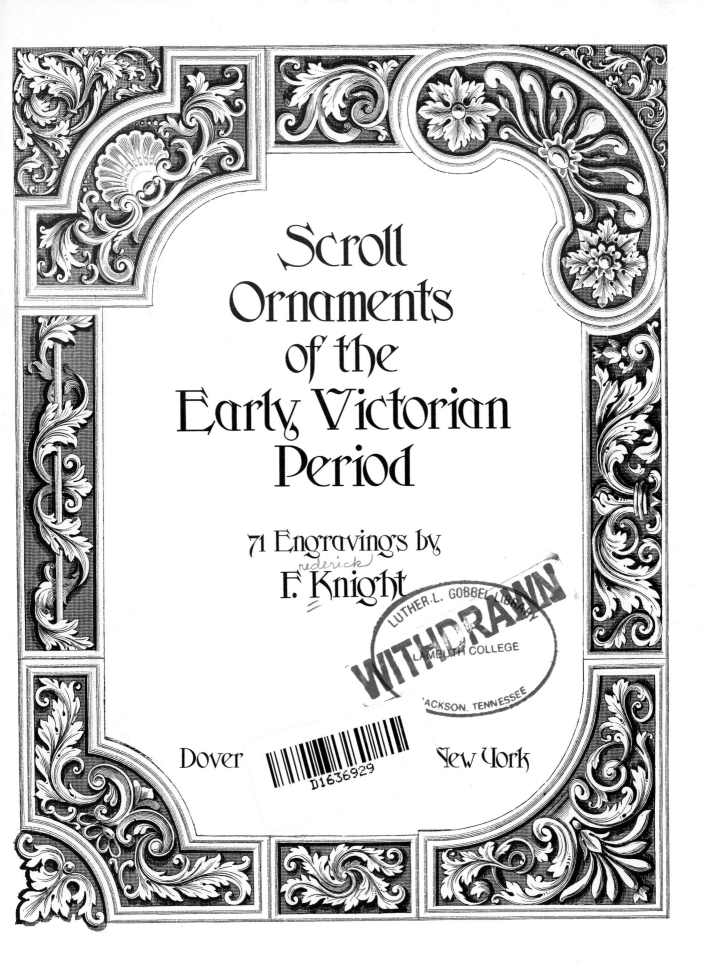

Scroll Ornaments of the Early Victorian Period

71 Engravings by

F. Knight

Dover   New York

Publisher's Note

The original source for this anthology, *Knight's Scroll Ornaments,* consisted of 50 engraved plates. Plate 1 was the title page (reproduced here on the page opposite to this); plate 50 was a framed engraving, "The Winds of AEolus," depicting the god of the winds surrounded by his subjects, a number of very unhappy cherub-like grotesques. The illustration has been removed, and the decorative border only is used to frame the title page of this reprint. The designs on the other 48 original plates appear in roughly the same order as before, although some plates have been recombined with other plates, thus reducing the total number of pages but losing none of the engravings. A fold-out instruction sheet describing the drawing and engraving of alphabets (presumably for use with the ornaments) has been dropped, and the original plate numbers have been replaced with new numbers for each design.

The original credit lines for each plate (not reproduced here) confirm that all but two of the plates were engraved by F. Knight—figure 71 of this edition was engraved by John Bacon, and figure 46 by R. Hebblethwaite. A number of different artists are credited for the designs, the most frequently encountered names being S. Ireton and J. Page. Since the original book does not even give a date of publication (although a handwritten inscription in the copy used for reproduction here is dated 1847), we are left with very little information about these artists. But at least three things can be said about Mr. F. Knight. First, he was a prolific engraver of similar material, as the list of his other collections on the original title page testifies. Second, he was well aware of the commercial nature of his work—note the advertisement for two of his other titles camouflaged in figure 38. Third, his engravings are excellent representations of the florid ornament that was to become a hallmark of Victorian design.

The changes made for the Dover edition are described in the Publisher's Note.

DOVER *Pictorial Archive* SERIES

Scroll Ornaments of the Early Victorian Period belongs to the Dover Pictorial Archive Series. Up to ten illustrations may be reproduced on any one project or in any single publication, free and without special permission. Wherever possible, include a credit line indicating the title of this book, author and publisher. Please address the publisher for permission to make more extensive use of illustrations in this book than that authorized above.

The reproduction of this book in whole is prohibited.

International Standard Book Number: 0-486-23596-3
Library of Congress Catalog Card Number: 77-88652

Manufactured in the United States of America
Dover Publications, Inc.
31 East 2nd Street
Mineola, N.Y. 11501

KNIGHT'S
Scroll Ornaments
Designed for the use of
Silversmiths, Chasers, Die-Sinkers,
MODELLERS, &c. &c.

The Writing by   J. H. Whiteman

S. Ireton Del.   **LONDON.**   F. Knight. Sc.

Published by J. Williams, 10. Charles Street, Soho.
T. Griffiths, 3. Wellington St. Strand, Ackerman &C° Strand.

Works Just Published by F. Knight.

Heraldic Illustrations, Quarto, 5 Parts. Price	0 . 4 . 0 each.
Book of Crests, 30 Quarto Plates	1 . 10 . 0
Modern & Antique Gems, 86 Plates	1 . 11 . 6

Vases & Ornaments 50 Quarto Plates 2.10.0.   Book of 758 Cyphers 12/.   Ornamental Alphabets 5 Quarto Plates 3/.

Fig. 3

Fig. 4

Fig. 5

Fig. 6

Fig. 7

Fig. 8

7

Fig. 9

Fig. 10

8

Fig. 11

Fig. 12

Fig. 13

9

Fig. 14

Fig. 15

11

Fig. 16

12

Fig. 17

13

Fig. 18

14

Fig. 19

Fig. 20

Fig. 21

15

Fig. 22

Fig. 23

Fig. 24

Fig. 25

16

Fig. 26

17

Fig. 27

Fig. 28

Fig. 29

Fig. 30

Fig. 31

Fig. 32

21

Fig. 33

Fig. 34

Fig. 35

24

Fig. 36

Fig. 37

Fig. 38

Fig. 39

Fig. 40

Fig. 41

Fig. 42

Fig. 43

Fig. 44

Fig. 45

29

R. Hobblethwaite Del et Sc.

The Gates at the Royal Lodge, Hyde Park Corner,
Cast by Messrs. Bramah & Son,
Being 21 Feet High by 16 Feet 9 Inches in Width, and Weighs 184. 1. 26.

Fig. 46

Fig. 47

Fig. 48

Fig. 49

Fig. 50

Fig. 51

Fig. 52

Fig. 53

Fig. 54

Fig. 55

Fig. 56

Fig. 57

Fig. 58

Fig. 59

37

Fig. 60

Fig. 61

Fig. 62

40

Fig. 63

Fig. 64

Fig. 65

Fig. 66

Fig. 67

45

Fig. 68

Fig. 69

Fig. 70

Fig. 71